LIFE ISN'T WHAT IT IS OR WHAT IT OFFERS: IT IS, WHAT YOU MAKE OF IT.

SKETA

Life is never just a piece of cake, Sometimes, it's just the fork

...Sketa

Focus is Everything!

...Sketa

DON'T
RIGHT

LIFE IS

CHANGE NEEDS CHANGE.

...SKETA

Focus is Everything!

...Sketa

EVERYDAY IS A BLESSED DAY.

...SKETA

IF YOU
JUST

YOU
DI

R THE
IE OR
U MAKE

EVERYDAY IS A BLESSED DAY.

...SKETA

LIFE'S NOT MOVIN', UNLESS IT'S MOVIN'!

...SKETA

Focus is Everything!

...Sketa

ams a

e in.

Sometimes,
in order to go
forward,
we need to work
out where we've
been.

Sketa

LIFE ROCKS!

...SKETA

PROVED
SON'S
ADE A
CE.

Focus is Everything!

...Sketa

LIVE A LIFE, NOT AN EXISTENCE.

...SKETA

Life is never just a piece of cake, sometimes, it's just the fork

Sketa

>LLWF<

Live Life Without Fear

is dedicated to
my late father who sadly
passed away from cancer, in
2014.

Like so many, his time was cut
short, but he lived, loved, and
laughed like no other I have
known.

Through his inspiration and my
creation, I pray I have honoured
his life and helped a million other
individuals to:

Live Life Without Fear

...as he continues to remind me
every day.

LILIWIOFE'

Live Life Without Fear

2022 LIFE DIARY

Published in Australia by
ELK PUBLISHING

PERSONAL INFORMATION

NAME

ADDRESS

MOBILE

E-MAIL

BUSINESS NAME

BUSINESS ADDRESS

BUSINESS PHONE

BUSINESS E-MAIL

BUEINESS WEBSITE

DRIVERS LICENCE

In case of accident please contact:
NAME

ADDRESS

PHONE

LLWF: Live Life Without Fear Diaries are specifically designed to motivate, inspire, energise, organise and realise that you can achieve so much more than you think you can and that you don't need to be afraid to ask the universe for your place among the stars.

LLWF: Live Life Without Fear

Published in Australia
by ELK Publishing

2022Planner

JANUARY

1
2
3
4
5
6
7
8
9
10
11
12
13
14
15
16
17
18
19
20
21
22
23
24
25
26
27
28
29
30
31

FEBRUARY

1
2
3
4
5
6
7
8
9
10
11
12
13
14
15
16
17
18
19
20
21
22
23
24
25
26
27
28
29

MARCH

1
2
3
4
5
6
7
8
9
10
11
12
13
14
15
16
17
18
19
20
21
22
23
24
25
26
27
28
29
30
31

JANUARY FEBRUARY MARCH

APRIL	MAY	JUNE
	1	1
	2	2
	3	3
	4	4
	5	5
	6	6
	7	7
	8	8
	9	9
0	10	10
1	11	11
2	12	12
3	13	13
4	14	14
5	15	15
6	16	16
7	17	17
8	18	18
9	19	19
0	20	20
1	21	21
2	22	22
3	23	23
4	24	24
5	25	25
6	26	26
7	27	27
8	28	28
9	29	29
0	30	30
	31	

APRIL MAY JUNE

2022 Planner

JULY	AUGUST	SEPTEMBER
1 ____	1 ____	1 ____
2 ____	2 ____	2 ____
3 ____	3 ____	3 ____
4 ____	4 ____	4 ____
5 ____	5 ____	5 ____
6 ____	6 ____	6 ____
7 ____	7 ____	7 ____
8 ____	8 ____	8 ____
9 ____	9 ____	9 ____
10 ____	10 ____	10 ____
11 ____	11 ____	11 ____
12 ____	12 ____	12 ____
13 ____	13 ____	13 ____
14 ____	14 ____	14 ____
15 ____	15 ____	15 ____
16 ____	16 ____	16 ____
17 ____	17 ____	17 ____
18 ____	18 ____	18 ____
19 ____	19 ____	19 ____
20 ____	20 ____	20 ____
21 ____	21 ____	21 ____
22 ____	22 ____	22 ____
23 ____	23 ____	23 ____
24 ____	24 ____	24 ____
25 ____	25 ____	25 ____
26 ____	26 ____	26 ____
27 ____	27 ____	27 ____
28 ____	28 ____	28 ____
29 ____	29 ____	29 ____
30 ____	30 ____	30 ____
31 ____	31 ____	

JULY AUGUST SEPTEMBER

OCTOBER	NOVEMBER	DECEMBER
1	1	1
2	2	2
3	3	3
4	4	4
5	5	5
6	6	6
7	7	7
8	8	8
9	9	9
10	10	10
11	11	11
12	12	12
13	13	13
14	14	14
15	15	15
16	16	16
17	17	17
18	18	18
19	19	19
20	20	20
21	21	21
22	22	22
23	23	23
24	24	24
25	25	25
26	26	26
27	27	27
28	28	28
29	29	29
30	30	30
31		

OCTOBER NOVEMBER DECEMBER

2022 CALENDAR

JANUARY						
M	T	W	T	F	S	S
31					1	2
3	4	5	6	7	8	9
10	11	12	13	14	15	16
17	18	19	20	21	22	23
24	25	26	27	28	29	30

FEBRUARY						
M	T	W	T	F	S	S
	1	2	3	4	5	6
7	8	9	10	11	12	13
14	15	16	17	18	19	20
21	22	23	24	25	26	27
28						

MARCH						
M	T	W	T	F	S	S
	1	2	3	4	5	6
7	8	9	10	11	12	13
14	15	16	17	18	19	20
21	22	23	24	25	26	27
28	29	30	31			

APRIL						
M	T	W	T	F	S	S
				1	2	3
4	5	6	7	8	9	10
11	12	13	14	15	16	17
18	19	20	21	22	23	24
25	26	27	28	29	30	

MAY						
M	T	W	T	F	S	S
30	31					1
2	3	4	5	6	7	8
9	10	11	12	13	14	15
16	17	18	19	20	21	22
23	24	25	26	27	28	29

JUNE						
M	T	W	T	F	S	S
		1	2	3	4	5
6	7	8	9	10	11	12
13	14	15	16	17	18	19
20	21	22	23	24	25	26
27	28	29	30			

2022 CALENDAR

JULY						
M	T	W	T	F	S	S
				1	2	3
4	5	6	7	8	9	10
11	12	13	14	15	16	17
18	19	20	21	22	23	24
25	26	27	28	29	30	31

AUGUST						
M	T	W	T	F	S	S
1	2	3	4	5	6	7
8	9	10	11	12	13	14
15	16	17	18	19	20	21
22	23	24	25	26	27	28
29	30	31				

SEPTEMBER						
M	T	W	T	F	S	S
			1	2	3	4
5	6	7	8	9	10	11
12	13	14	15	16	17	18
19	20	21	22	23	24	25
26	27	28	29	30		

OCTOBER						
M	T	W	T	F	S	S
31					1	2
3	4	5	6	7	8	9
10	11	12	13	14	15	16
17	18	19	20	21	22	23
24	25	26	27	28	29	30

NOVEMBER						
M	T	W	T	F	S	S
	1	2	3	4	5	6
7	8	9	10	11	12	13
14	15	16	17	18	19	20
21	22	23	24	25	26	27
28	29	30				

DECEMBER						
M	T	W	T	F	S	S
			1	2	3	4
5	6	7	8	9	10	11
12	13	14	15	16	17	18
19	20	21	22	23	24	25
26	27	28	29	30	31	

PUBLIC HOLIDAYS 2022

WORLD OBSERVATIONS

Jan 1 - New Year's Day (Jan 3 New Year's Holiday)
Dec 25 - Christmas Day
Dec 26 - Boxing Day
Dec 27 - Christmas Day Holiday

AUSTRALIA

Jan 26 - Australian Day
Jan 26 - Australia Day Holiday
Mar 14 - Labour Day (ACT)
Apr 15 - Good Friday
Apr 16 - Easter Saturday
Apr 17 - Easter Sunday
Apr 18 - Easter Monday
April 25 - Anzac Day
May 2 - Labour Day (QLD)
Jun 13 - Queens Birthday Holiday (Oct 3 - Qld & 26 Sept - WA)
Dec 26 - Boxing Day Holiday

NEW ZEALAND

Feb 1 - Auckland Anniversary
Feb 6 - Waitangi Day
Apr 15- Good Friday
Apr 18 - Easter Monday
April 25 - Anzac Day
Jun 6 - Queen's Birthday
Oct 24 - Labour Day

UNITED KINGDOM

May 1 - Labour Day
May 2 - May Day
Jun 2 - Late May Bank Holiday
Jun 13 Queens Birthday (Platinum Jubilee)
Aug 29 - Bank Holiday
Nov 30 - St Andrew's Day
Dec 26 - Boxing Day Holiday

USA

Jan 17 - Martin Luther King Jr. Day
Feb 21- Presidents' Day
Apr 15 - Emancipation Day
May 30 - Memorial Day
Jul 4 - Independence Day Holiday
Oct 10 - Columbus Day
Nov 11 - Veterans Day
Nov 24 - Thanks Giving Day

FRANCE & GERMANY

May 8 - Victory Day
May 26 - Ascension Day
Jun 5 & 6 - Whit Sunday & Mon
Jul 14 - Bastille Day
Nov 1 - All Saints' Day
Nov 11 - Armistice Day

GERMANY

Aug 15 - Assumption Day
Jun 3 - Corpus Christi
Oct 3 - German Unity
Oct 31 - Reformation Day

PUBLIC HOLIDAYS 2022

ASIAN OBSERVATIONS
Feb 1-3 - Chinese Lunar New Year
May 8 - Buddha's Birthday

HONG KONG/CHINA
Jul 1 - HKSAR (Establishment Day)
Feb 1 - Lattern Festival (15th Day of Month 1 - Lunar calendar)
Apr 5 - Qing Ming Jie(Tomb Sweeping Festival)
Apr 15 - Good Friday
Apr 16 - Easter Saturday
Apr 18 - Easter Monday
May 1 - Labour Day
June 3 - (Tuen Ng) Dragon Boat Festival
Sept 10 - Mid-Autumn Festival
Oct 1 - National Day
Oct 4 - Chung Yeung Festival & holiday

KOREA
Jan 31~Feb 2 - SolNal (Korean New Year)
Mar 1 - March 1st Movement Day
May 8 - Buddha's Birthday
May 5 - Children's Day
Jun 6 - Memorial Day
Aug 15 - Liberation Day
Sept 9~11 - Chusok (Korean Thanks Giving)
Oct 3 - National Foundation Day
Oct 9 - Hangeul Day
Dec 25 - Christmas Day

LLWF BUCKET LIST

- [ ]
- [ ]
- [ ]
- [ ]
- [ ]
- [ ]
- [ ]
- [ ]
- [ ]
- [ ]
- [ ]
- [ ]
- [ ]
- [ ]
- [ ]
- [ ]
- [ ]
- [ ]
- [ ]
- [ ]

LLWF NOTES

- [ ]
- [ ]
- [ ]
- [ ]
- [ ]
- [ ]
- [ ]
- [ ]
- [ ]
- [ ]
- [ ]
- [ ]
- [ ]
- [ ]
- [ ]
- [ ]
- [ ]
- [ ]
- [ ]
- [ ]

LLWF TO DO LIST

- [ ]
- [ ]
- [ ]
- [ ]
- [ ]
- [ ]
- [ ]
- [ ]
- [ ]
- [ ]
- [ ]
- [ ]
- [ ]
- [ ]
- [ ]
- [ ]
- [ ]
- [ ]
- [ ]
- [ ]

LLWF TO DO LIST

Monday | 월요일 | Lundi | 星期一 | Montag 27

EVERYDAY IS A BLESSED DAY.
...SKETA

#MustDoMonday

Tuesday | 화요일 | Mardi | 星期二 | Dienstag 28

#TimeTravelTuesday

Wednesday | 수요일 | Mercredi | 星期三 | Mittwoch 29

#WednesdayWishes

30 Thursday | 목요일 | Jeidi | 星期四 | Donnerstag

#ThinkThursday

31 Friday | 금요일 | Vendredi | 星期五 | Freitag

#FameFriday

Saturday | 토요일
Samedi | 星期六 | Samstag 1

#SaveSaturday

Sunday | 일요일
2 Dimanche | 星期日 | Sonntag

#SelinaSunday

Monday | 월요일 | Lundi | 星期一 | Montag

3

Build your dreams a reality to live in.

Sketa

#MakeItMonday

Tuesday | 화요일 | Mardi | 星期二 | Dienstag

4

#TeamTuesday

Wednesday | 수요일 | Mercredi | 星期三 | Mittwoch

5

#WCW

6

Thursday | 목요일 | Jeidi | 星期四 | Donnerstag

#ThursdayThanks

7

Friday | 금요일 | Vendredi | 星期五 | Freitag

#FamFriday

Saturday | 토요일
Samedi | 星期六 | Samstag

8

#SaturdaySun

9

Sunday | 일요일
Dimanche | 星期日 | Sonntag

#SoulSunday

Monday | 월요일 | Lundi | 星期一 | Montag 10

Time is energy, but energy gives time worth.

Sketa

#MoveMonday

Tuesday | 화요일 | Mardi | 星期二 | Dienstag 11

#TTTuesday

Wednesday | 수요일 | Mercredi | 星期三 | Mittwoch 12

#WriteWednesday

13

Thursday | 목요일 | Jeidi | 星期四 | Donnerstag

#ThoughtfulThursday

14

Friday | 금요일 | Vendredi | 星期五 | Freitag

#FlyFriday

Saturday | 토요일
Samedi | 星期六 | Samstag

15

#SuperSaturday

16

Sunday | 일요일
Dimanche | 星期日 | Sonntag

#SavourSunday

Monday | 월요일 | Lundi | 星期一 | Montag

17

Don't wait for the right day, time or year.
Life is what you make it
NOW!
...Sketa

#MentorMonday

Tuesday | 화요일 | Mardi | 星期二 | Dienstag

18

#TeaTuesday

Wednesday | 수요일 | Mercredi | 星期三 | Mittwoch

19

#watercolour

20

Thursday | 목요일 | Jeidi | 星期四 | Donnerstag

#TeachThursday

21

Friday | 금요일 | Vendredi | 星期五 | Freitag

#FunFriday

Saturday | 토요일
Samedi | 星期六 | Samstag

22

#SketchSaturday

23

Sunday | 일요일
Dimanche | 星期日 | Sonntag

#SillySunday

Monday | 월요일 | Lundi | 星期一 | Montag 24

Dreams vs Reality

Šketa

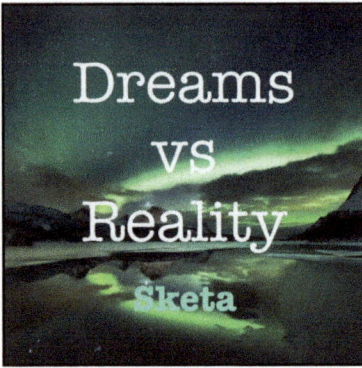

#MotivateMonday

Tuesday | 화요일 | Mardi | 星期二 | Dienstag 25

#TheatreTuesday

Wednesday | 수요일 | Mercredi | 星期三 | Mittwoch 26

#WorldWednesday

27

Thursday | 목요일 | Jeidi | 星期四 | Donnerstag

#TravelThursday

28

Friday | 금요일 | Vendredi | 星期五 | Freitag

#FilmFriday

Saturday | 토요일
Samedi | 星期六 | Samstag

29

#SexySaturday

30

Sunday | 일요일
Dimanche | 星期日 | Sonntag

#SleepSunday

JANUARY

Monday | 월요일 | Lundi | 星期一 | Montag 31

You don't have to reinvent the wheel, just improve on it!

Sketa

#MeMonday

Tuesday | 화요일 | Mardi | 星期二 | Dienstag 1

#TrumpTuesday

Wednesday | 수요일 | Mercredi | 星期三 | Mittwoch 2

#WatchMeWednesday

3

Thursday | 목요일 | Jeidi | 星期四 | Donnerstag

#TogetherThursday

4

Friday | 금요일 | Vendredi | 星期五 | Freitag

#FrameFriday

Saturday | 토요일
Samedi | 星期六 | Samstag

5

#ShopSaturday

6

Sunday | 일요일
Dimanche | 星期日 | Sonntag

#SpiritSunday

Monday | 월요일 | Lundi | 星期一 | Montag

7

Life's full of trial and error, but you've got to get it right. Ironic.

Sketa

#MysteryMonday

Tuesday | 화요일 | Mardi | 星期二 | Dienstag

8

#TellAllTuesday

Wednesday | 수요일 | Mercredi | 星期三 | Mittwoch

9

#WiggleWednesday

10 Thursday | 목요일 | Jeidi | 星期四 | Donnerstag

#ToDoThursday

11 Friday | 금요일 | Vendredi | 星期五 | Freitag

#FatherFriday

Saturday | 토요일
Samedi | 星期六 | Samstag 12

#SportSaturday

13 Sunday | 일요일
Dimanche | 星期日 | Sonntag

#SongSunday

Monday | 월요일 | Lundi | 星期一 | Montag 14

LIFE ISN'T WHAT IT IS OR WHAT IT OFFERS: IT IS, WHAT YOU MAKE OF IT.

SKETA

#MotherMonday

Tuesday | 화요일 | Mardi | 星期二 | Dienstag 15

#TryTuesday

Wednesday | 수요일 | Mercredi | 星期三 | Mittwoch 16

#WarriorWednesday

17 Thursday | 목요일 | Jeidi | 星期四 | Donnerstag

#ThrowbackThursday

18 Friday | 금요일 | Vendredi | 星期五 | Freitag

#FriendsFriday

Saturday | 토요일
Samedi | 星期六 | Samstag 19

#ShoutoutSaturday

Sunday | 일요일
20 Dimanche | 星期日 | Sonntag

#SacrificeSunday

FEBRUARY

Monday | 월요일 | Lundi | 星期一 | Montag

21

success
=
hard yakka +
blisters

Sketa

#MustDoMonday

Tuesday | 화요일 | Mardi | 星期二 | Dienstag

22

#TimeTravelTuesday

Wednesday | 수요일 | Mercredi | 星期三 | Mittwoch

23

#WednesdayWishes

24

Thursday | 목요일 | Jeidi | 星期四 | Donnerstag

#ThinkThursday

25

Friday | 금요일 | Vendredi | 星期五 | Freitag

#FameFriday

Saturday | 토요일
Samedi | 星期六 | Samstag

26

#SaveSaturday

27

Sunday | 일요일
Dimanche | 星期日 | Sonntag

#SelinaSunday

Monday | 월요일 | Lundi | 星期一 | Montag 28

Inequality is not born out of circumstance.
It is born out of narrow-minded individuals;
Who thrive on bully mentality,
Who can not see past their own insecurities.

...Sketa

#MakeItMonday

Tuesday | 화요일 | Mardi | 星期二 | Dienstag 1

#TeamTuesday

Wednesday | 수요일 | Mercredi | 星期三 | Mittwoch 2

#WCW

3

Thursday | 목요일 | Jeidi | 星期四 | Donnerstag

#ThursdayThanks

4

Friday | 금요일 | Vendredi | 星期五 | Freitag

#FamFriday

Saturday | 토요일
Samedi | 星期六 | Samstag

5

#SaturdaySun

6

Sunday | 일요일
Dimanche | 星期日 | Sonntag

#SoulSunday

Monday | 월요일 | Lundi | 星期一 | Montag 7

PATIENCE IS OFTEN BUILT ON THE BACK OF PROBLEMS OF OTHERS.

...SKETA

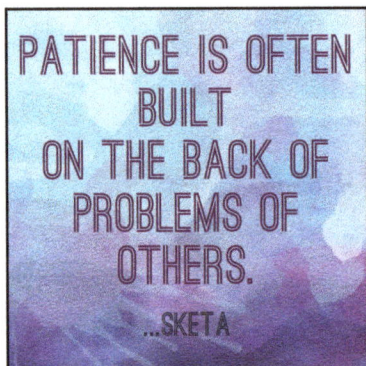

#MentorMonday

Tuesday | 화요일 | Mardi | 星期二 | Dienstag 8

#TeaTuesday

Wednesday | 수요일 | Mercredi | 星期三 | Mittwoch 9

#Watercolour

10 Thursday | 목요일 | Jeidi | 星期四 | Donnerstag

#TeachThursday

11 Friday | 금요일 | Vendredi | 星期五 | Freitag

#FunFriday

Saturday | 토요일
Samedi | 星期六 | Samstag 12

#SketchSaturday

Sunday | 일요일
13 Dimanche | 星期日 | Sonntag

#SillySunday

Monday | 월요일 | Lundi | 星期一 | Montag

14

Life is never just a piece of cake, sometimes, it's just the fork

...Sketa

#MotivateMonday

Tuesday | 화요일 | Mardi | 星期二 | Dienstag

15

#TheatreTuesday

Wednesday | 수요일 | Mercredi | 星期三 | Mittwoch

16

#WorldWednesday

17 Thursday | 목요일 | Jeidi | 星期四 | Donnerstag

#TravelThursday

18 Friday | 금요일 | Vendredi | 星期五 | Freitag

#FilmFriday

Saturday | 토요일
Samedi | 星期六 | Samstag **19**

#SexySaturday

Sunday | 일요일
20 Dimanche | 星期日 | Sonntag

#SleepSunday

Monday | 월요일 | Lundi | 星期一 | Montag 21

It's never too late to put a dream in motion!

...Sketa

#MentorMonday

Tuesday | 화요일 | Mardi | 星期二 | Dienstag 22

#TeaTuesday

Wednesday | 수요일 | Mercredi | 星期三 | Mittwoch 23

#watercolour

24 Thursday | 목요일 | Jeidi | 星期四 | Donnerstag

#TeachThursday

25 Friday | 금요일 | Vendredi | 星期五 | Freitag

#FunFriday

Saturday | 토요일
Samedi | 星期六 | Samstag 26

#SketchSaturday

27 Sunday | 일요일
Dimanche | 星期日 | Sonntag

#SillySunday

Monday | 월요일 | Lundi | 星期一 | Montag

28

SUCCESS
=
HOW MUCH YOU WANT IT
+
HOW HARD YOU WILL WORK
TO GET IT!
...SKETA

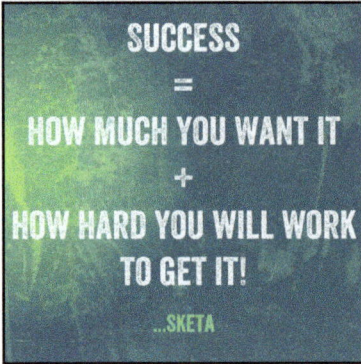

#MakeItMonday

Tuesday | 화요일 | Mardi | 星期二 | Dienstag

29

#TeamTuesday

Wednesday | 수요일 | Mercredi | 星期三 | Mittwoch

30

#WCW

31 Thursday | 목요일 | Jeidi | 星期四 | Donnerstag

#ThursdayThanks

1 Friday | 금요일 | Vendredi | 星期五 | Freitag

#FamFriday

Saturday | 토요일
Samedi | 星期六 | Samstag 2

#SaturdaySun

Sunday | 일요일
3 Dimanche | 星期日 | Sonntag

#SoulSunday

APRIL

Monday | 월요일 | Lundi | 星期一 | Montag

4

THERE IS NO GETTING OLDER, FOR IF THE CELLULAR STRUCTURE DIES OFF AND REPLACES ITSELF IN TOTAL BY THE END OF THE 2ND MONTH - WE ARE THEN A NEW PERSON.

NOT WHAT WE ARE OR WHAT WE WERE - BUT A NEW PERSON WITH A NEW BEING AND A NEW START ON LIFE.

...SKETA

#MoveMonday

Tuesday | 화요일 | Mardi | 星期二 | Dienstag

5

#TTTuesday

Wednesday | 수요일 | Mercredi | 星期三 | Mittwoch

6

#WriteWednesday

7

Thursday | 목요일 | Jeidi | 星期四 | Donnerstag

#ThoughtfulThursday

8

Friday | 금요일 | Vendredi | 星期五 | Freitag

#FlyFriday

Saturday | 토요일
Samedi | 星期六 | Samstag

9

#SuperSaturday

Sunday | 일요일

10

Dimanche | 星期日 | Sonntag

#SavourSunday

APRIL

Monday | 월요일 | Lundi | 星期一 | Montag 11

GOALS...
TO BE BETTER THAN I WAS YESTERDAY; MORE FOCUSED THAN I WAS A MINUTE AGO; MORE RESILIENT THAN I WAS A YEAR AGO.
TO ACHIEVE MORE THAN I DID YESTERDAY; CREATE MORE THAN I DID A MINUTE AGO; SUCCEED WHERE I FAILED A YEAR AGO.
SKETA

#MentorMonday

Tuesday | 화요일 | Mardi | 星期二 | Dienstag 12

#TeaTuesday

Wednesday | 수요일 | Mercredi | 星期三 | Mittwoch 13

#Watercolour

14

Thursday | 목요일 | Jeidi | 星期四 | Donnerstag

#TeachThursday

15

Friday | 금요일 | Vendredi | 星期五 | Freitag

#FunFriday

Saturday | 토요일
Samedi | 星期六 | Samstag

16

#SketchSaturday

17

Sunday | 일요일
Dimanche | 星期日 | Sonntag

#SillySunday

Monday | 월요일 | Lundi | 星期一 | Montag 18

To be fickle - is to live a life without commitment, without honour, without depth of honesty or integrity. Yes, to be shallow - even on social media.

Sketa

#MotivateMonday

Tuesday | 화요일 | Mardi | 星期二 | Dienstag 19

#TheatreTuesday

Wednesday | 수요일 | Mercredi | 星期三 | Mittwoch 20

#WorldWednesday

21 Thursday | 목요일 | Jeidi | 星期四 | Donnerstag

#TravelThursday

22 Friday | 금요일 | Vendredi | 星期五 | Freitag

#FilmFriday

Saturday | 토요일
Samedi | 星期六 | Samstag 23

#SexySaturday

Sunday | 일요일
24 Dimanche | 星期日 | Sonntag

#SleepSunday

Monday | 월요일 | Lundi | 星期一 | Montag

25

CARING FOR OUR WORLD IS EVERYONE'S RESPONSIBILITY.
...SKETA

#MeMonday

Tuesday | 화요일 | Mardi | 星期二 | Dienstag

26

#TrumpTuesday

Wednesday | 수요일 | Mercredi | 星期三 | Mittwoch

27

#WatchMeWednesday

28

Thursday | 목요일 | Jeidi | 星期四 | Donnerstag

#TogetherThursday

29

Friday | 금요일 | Vendredi | 星期五 | Freitag

#FrameFriday

Saturday | 토요일
Samedi | 星期六 | Samstag

30

#ShopSaturday

1

Sunday | 일요일
Dimanche | 星期日 | Sonntag

#SpiritSunday

MAY

Monday | 월요일 | Lundi | 星期一 | Montag

2

You can never be old and wise if you were never young and crazy...

Sketa

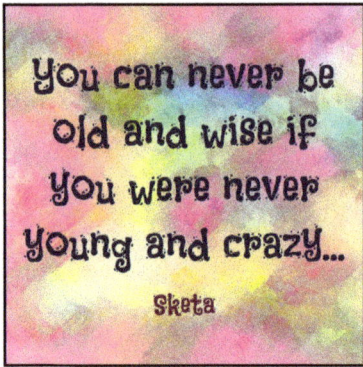

#MysteryMonday

Tuesday | 화요일 | Mardi | 星期二 | Dienstag

3

#TellAllTuesday

Wednesday | 수요일 | Mercredi | 星期三 | Mittwoch

4

#WiggleWednesday

5 Thursday | 목요일 | Jeidi | 星期四 | Donnerstag

#ToDoThursday

6 Friday | 금요일 | Vendredi | 星期五 | Freitag

#FatherFriday

Saturday | 토요일
Samedi | 星期六 | Samstag 7

#SportSaturday

8 Sunday | 일요일
Dimanche | 星期日 | Sonntag

#SongSunday

Monday | 월요일 | Lundi | 星期一 | Montag 9

Your thoughts are a reflection of **education.**
Your behaviour is a reflection of your **thoughts.**
Your treatment of others is a reflection of your **self worth.**
...Sketa

#MotherMonday

Tuesday | 화요일 | Mardi | 星期二 | Dienstag 10

#TryTuesday

Wednesday | 수요일 | Mercredi | 星期三 | Mittwoch 11

#WarriorWednesday

12

Thursday | 목요일 | Jeidi | 星期四 | Donnerstag

#ThrowbackThursday

13

Friday | 금요일 | Vendredi | 星期五 | Freitag

#FriendsFriday

Saturday | 토요일
Samedi | 星期六 | Samstag

14

#ShoutoutSaturday

15

Sunday | 일요일
Dimanche | 星期日 | Sonntag

#SacrificeSunday

Monday | 월요일 | Lundi | 星期一 | Montag

16

THE DEFINITION OF TRUE FRIENDSHIP IS:

BELIEVING IN YOU WITHOUT QUESTION;
SUPPORTING YOU WITHOUT FAIL;
HOLDING YOU UP WHEN YOUR WORLD COMES CRASHING DOWN;
LOVING YOU - FLAWS AND ALL.

TELLING YOU WHEN YOU'RE WRONG;
SAYING, "YOU CAN BE STRONG!"
TREATING YOU WITH EQUAL RESPECT & UNDERSTANDING;
ALWAYS BEING THERE FOR YOUR HAPPY LANDING.

...SEETA

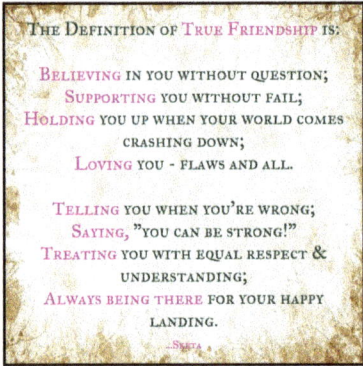

#MustDoMonday

Tuesday | 화요일 | Mardi | 星期二 | Dienstag

17

#TimeTravelTuesday

Wednesday | 수요일 | Mercredi | 星期三 | Mittwoch

18

#WednesdayWishes

19 Thursday | 목요일 | Jeidi | 星期四 | Donnerstag

#ThinkThursday

20 Friday | 금요일 | Vendredi | 星期五 | Freitag

#FameFriday

Saturday | 토요일
Samedi | 星期六 | Samstag 21

#SaveSaturday

22 Sunday | 일요일
Dimanche | 星期日 | Sonntag

#SelinaSunday

Monday | 월요일 | Lundi | 星期一 | Montag

23

LOVE
=
COMPROMISE
+
TRUST
+
UNDERSTANDING
+
FORGIVENESS
...SKETA

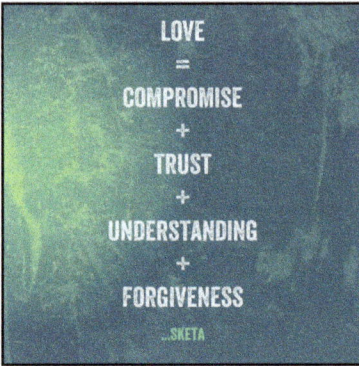

#MakeItMonday

Tuesday | 화요일 | Mardi | 星期二 | Dienstag

24

#TeamTuesday

Wednesday | 수요일 | Mercredi | 星期三 | Mittwoch

25

#WCW

26 Thursday | 목요일 | Jeidi | 星期四 | Donnerstag

#ThursdayThanks

27 Friday | 금요일 | Vendredi | 星期五 | Freitag

#FamFriday

Saturday | 토요일
Samedi | 星期六 | Samstag 28

#SaturdaySun

29 Sunday | 일요일
Dimanche | 星期日 | Sonntag

#SoulSunday

Monday | 월요일 | Lundi | 星期一 | Montag

30

SOMETIMES, THE PLACE YOU GET USED TO, IS NOT THE PLACE YOU BELONG.
YOU BELONG, WHERE YOU THINK YOU BELONG.
WHERE DO YOU BELONG?

SKETA

#MoveMonday

Tuesday | 화요일 | Mardi | 星期二 | Dienstag

31

#TTTuesday

Wednesday | 수요일 | Mercredi | 星期三 | Mittwoch

1

#WriteWednesday

2

Thursday | 목요일 | Jeidi | 星期四 | Donnerstag

#ThoughtfulThursday

3

Friday | 금요일 | Vendredi | 星期五 | Freitag

#FlyFriday

Saturday | 토요일
Samedi | 星期六 | Samstag

4

#SuperSaturday

5

Sunday | 일요일
Dimanche | 星期日 | Sonntag

#SavourSunday

JUNE

Monday | 월요일 | Lundi | 星期一 | Montag

6

There is no such thing as being lost. if you know where your feet stand. where your heart beats and your head lies. there is no lost – only direction to be sought to see where you grow best!

...Sketa

#MentorMonday

Tuesday | 화요일 | Mardi | 星期二 | Dienstag

7

#TeaTuesday

Wednesday | 수요일 | Mercredi | 星期三 | Mittwoch

8

#Watercolour

9 Thursday | 목요일 | Jeidi | 星期四 | Donnerstag

#TeachThursday

10 Friday | 금요일 | Vendredi | 星期五 | Freitag

#FunFriday

Saturday | 토요일
Samedi | 星期六 | Samstag 11

#SketchSaturday

Sunday | 일요일
12 Dimanche | 星期日 | Sonntag

#SillySunday

Monday | 월요일 | Lundi | 星期一 | Montag

13

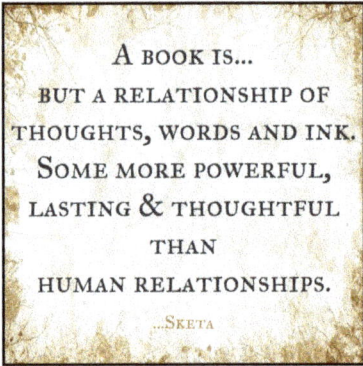

A BOOK IS...
BUT A RELATIONSHIP OF
THOUGHTS, WORDS AND INK.
SOME MORE POWERFUL,
LASTING & THOUGHTFUL
THAN
HUMAN RELATIONSHIPS.

...SKETA

#MotivateMonday

Tuesday | 화요일 | Mardi | 星期二 | Dienstag

14

#TheatreTuesday

Wednesday | 수요일 | Mercredi | 星期三 | Mittwoch

15

#WorldWednesday

16

Thursday | 목요일 | Jeidi | 星期四 | Donnerstag

#TravelThursday

17

Friday | 금요일 | Vendredi | 星期五 | Freitag

#FilmFriday

Saturday | 토요일
Samedi | 星期六 | Samstag

18

#SexySaturday

19

Sunday | 일요일
Dimanche | 星期日 | Sonntag

#SleepSunday

Monday | 월요일 | Lundi | 星期一 | Montag

20

LIFE IS NOT ABOUT DOING ENOUGH TO GET BY - JUST TO RECEIVE A PAYCHECK OR TO PLEASE ONE'S BOSS.
IT'S ABOUT DOING EVERYTHING TO THE BEST OF ONE'S ABILITY, SO YOU CAN BE PROUD OF YOURSELF AT THE END OF THE DAY - NO QUESTIONS ASKED.

SKETA

#MeMonday

Tuesday | 화요일 | Mardi | 星期二 | Dienstag

21

#TrumpTuesday

Wednesday | 수요일 | Mercredi | 星期三 | Mittwoch

22

#WatchMeWednesday

23 Thursday | 목요일 | Jeidi | 星期四 | Donnerstag

#TogetherThursday

24 Friday | 금요일 | Vendredi | 星期五 | Freitag

#FrameFriday

Saturday | 토요일
Samedi | 星期六 | Samstag 25

#ShopSaturday

Sunday | 일요일
26 Dimanche | 星期日 | Sonntag

#SpiritSunday

Monday | 월요일 | Lundi | 星期一 | Montag

27

CHANGE NEEDS CHANGE.

...SKETA

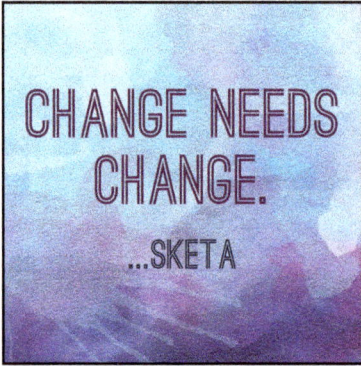

#MysteryMonday

Tuesday | 화요일 | Mardi | 星期二 | Dienstag

28

#TellAllTuesday

Wednesday | 수요일 | Mercredi | 星期三 | Mittwoch

29

#WiggleWednesday

30 Thursday | 목요일 | Jeidi | 星期四 | Donnerstag

#ToDoThursday

1 Friday | 금요일 | Vendredi | 星期五 | Freitag

#FatherFriday

Saturday | 토요일
Samedi | 星期六 | Samstag 2

#SportSaturday

3 Sunday | 일요일
Dimanche | 星期日 | Sonntag

#SongSunday

Monday | 월요일 | Lundi | 星期一 | Montag 4

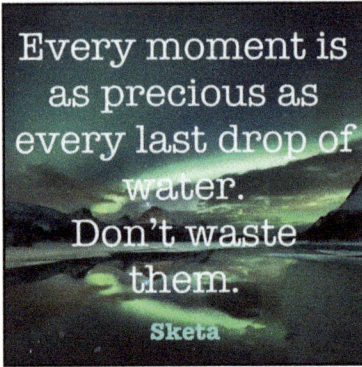

Every moment is as precious as every last drop of water. Don't waste them.
Sketa

#MotherMonday

Tuesday | 화요일 | Mardi | 星期二 | Dienstag 5

#TryTuesday

Wednesday | 수요일 | Mercredi | 星期三 | Mittwoch 6

#WarriorWednesday

7

Thursday | 목요일 | Jeidi | 星期四 | Donnerstag

#ThrowbackThursday

8

Friday | 금요일 | Vendredi | 星期五 | Freitag

#FriendsFriday

Saturday | 토요일
Samedi | 星期六 | Samstag

9

#ShoutoutSaturday

10

Sunday | 일요일
Dimanche | 星期日 | Sonntag

#SacrificeSunday

Monday | 월요일 | Lundi | 星期一 | Montag

11

Focus is Everything!

...Sketa

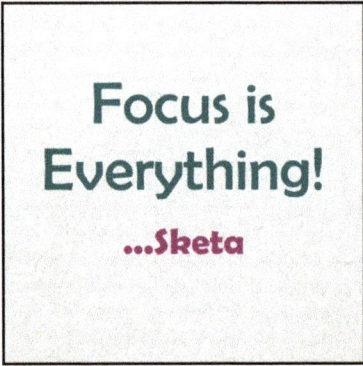

#MustDoMonday

Tuesday | 화요일 | Mardi | 星期二 | Dienstag

12

#TimeTravelTuesday

Wednesday | 수요일 | Mercredi | 星期三 | Mittwoch

13

#WednesdayWishes

14 Thursday | 목요일 | Jeidi | 星期四 | Donnerstag

#ThinkThursday

15 Friday | 금요일 | Vendredi | 星期五 | Freitag

#FameFriday

Saturday | 토요일
Samedi | 星期六 | Samstag 16

#SaveSaturday

17 Sunday | 일요일
Dimanche | 星期日 | Sonntag

#SelinaSunday

Monday | 월요일 | Lundi | 星期一 | Montag

18

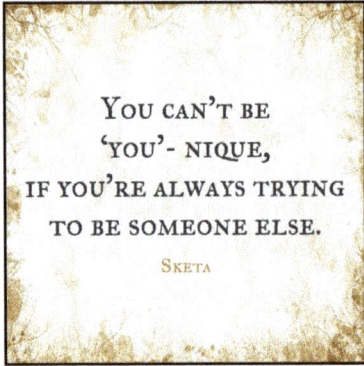

YOU CAN'T BE
'YOU'- NIQUE,
IF YOU'RE ALWAYS TRYING
TO BE SOMEONE ELSE.

SKETA

#MakeItMonday

Tuesday | 화요일 | Mardi | 星期二 | Dienstag

19

#TeamTuesday

Wednesday | 수요일 | Mercredi | 星期三 | Mittwoch

20

#WCW

21 Thursday | 목요일 | Jeidi | 星期四 | Donnerstag

#ThursdayThanks

22 Friday | 금요일 | Vendredi | 星期五 | Freitag

#FamFriday

Saturday | 토요일
Samedi | 星期六 | Samstag 23

#SaturdaySun

Sunday | 일요일
24 Dimanche | 星期日 | Sonntag

#SoulSunday

Monday | 월요일 | Lundi | 星期一 | Montag

25

Just COMMIT to becoming a better 'YOU'

...Sketa

#MoveMonday

Tuesday | 화요일 | Mardi | 星期二 | Dienstag

26

#TTTuesday

Wednesday | 수요일 | Mercredi | 星期三 | Mittwoch

27

#WriteWednesday

28

Thursday | 목요일 | Jeidi | 星期四 | Donnerstag

#ThoughtfulThursday

29

Friday | 금요일 | Vendredi | 星期五 | Freitag

#FlyFriday

Saturday | 토요일
Samedi | 星期六 | Samstag

30

#SuperSaturday

Sunday | 일요일

31

Dimanche | 星期日 | Sonntag

#SavourSunday

AUGUST

Monday | 월요일 | Lundi | 星期一 | Montag

1

IF YOU HAVE IMPROVED, JUST ONE PERSON'S LIFE, YOU HAVE MADE A DIFFERENCE.

...SKETA

#MentorMonday

Tuesday | 화요일 | Mardi | 星期二 | Dienstag

2

#TeaTuesday

Wednesday | 수요일 | Mercredi | 星期三 | Mittwoch

3

#Watercolour

4 Thursday | 목요일 | Jeidi | 星期四 | Donnerstag

#TeachThursday

5 Friday | 금요일 | Vendredi | 星期五 | Freitag

#FunFriday

Saturday | 토요일
Samedi | 星期六 | Samstag 6

#SketchSaturday

Sunday | 일요일
7 Dimanche | 星期日 | Sonntag

#SillySunday

AUGUST

Monday | 월요일 | Lundi | 星期一 | Montag

8

I love life!
Life loves me!
Life and I have a
wonderful spree!
...Sketa

#MotivateMonday

Tuesday | 화요일 | Mardi | 星期二 | Dienstag

9

#TheatreTuesday

Wednesday | 수요일 | Mercredi | 星期三 | Mittwoch

10

#WorldWednesday

11

Thursday | 목요일 | Jeidi | 星期四 | Donnerstag

#TravelThursday

12

Friday | 금요일 | Vendredi | 星期五 | Freitag

#FilmFriday

Saturday | 토요일
Samedi | 星期六 | Samstag

13

#SexySaturday

14

Sunday | 일요일
Dimanche | 星期日 | Sonntag

#SleepSunday

AUGUST

Monday | 월요일 | Lundi | 星期一 | Montag

15

YOU DON'T HAVE TO BE GREAT TO GET STARTED, BUT YOU HAVE TO GET STARTED TO BE GREAT!

SKETA

#MeMonday

Tuesday | 화요일 | Mardi | 星期二 | Dienstag

16

#TrumpTuesday

Wednesday | 수요일 | Mercredi | 星期三 | Mittwoch

17

#WatchMeWednesday

18

Thursday | 목요일 | Jeidi | 星期四 | Donnerstag

#TogetherThursday

19

Friday | 금요일 | Vendredi | 星期五 | Freitag

#FrameFriday

Saturday | 토요일
Samedi | 星期六 | Samstag

20

#ShopSaturday

21

Sunday | 일요일
Dimanche | 星期日 | Sonntag

#SpiritSunday

AUGUST

Monday | 월요일 | Lundi | 星期一 | Montag

22

LIVE A LIFE, NOT AN EXISTENCE.
...SKETA

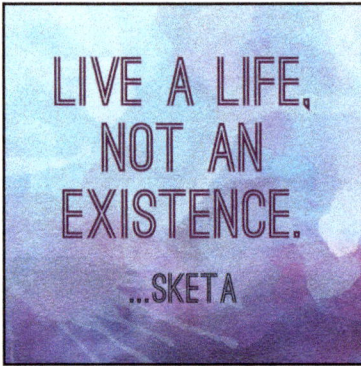

#MysteryMonday

Tuesday | 화요일 | Mardi | 星期二 | Dienstag

23

#TellAllTuesday

Wednesday | 수요일 | Mercredi | 星期三 | Mittwoch

24

#WiggleWednesday

25

Thursday | 목요일 | Jeidi | 星期四 | Donnerstag

#ToDoThursday

26

Friday | 금요일 | Vendredi | 星期五 | Freitag

#FatherFriday

Saturday | 토요일
Samedi | 星期六 | Samstag

27

#SportSaturday

28

Sunday | 일요일
Dimanche | 星期日 | Sonntag

#SongSunday

AUGUST

Monday | 월요일 | Lundi | 星期一 | Montag 29

Never let your work define you; You define your work.

...Sketa

#MotherMonday

Tuesday | 화요일 | Mardi | 星期二 | Dienstag 30

#TryTuesday

Wednesday | 수요일 | Mercredi | 星期三 | Mittwoch 31

#WarriorWednesday

1 Thursday | 목요일 | Jeidi | 星期四 | Donnerstag

#ThrowbackThursday

2 Friday | 금요일 | Vendredi | 星期五 | Freitag

#FriendsFriday

Saturday | 토요일
Samedi | 星期六 | Samstag 3

#ShoutoutSaturday

4 Sunday | 일요일
Dimanche | 星期日 | Sonntag

#SacrificeSunday

SEPTEMBER

Monday | 월요일 | Lundi | 星期一 | Montag

5

SOMETIMES, LIFE'S HARDER THAN YOU EXPECT. MORE THAN YOU DESERVE. A GREATER CHALLENGE THAN YOU ANTICIPATE.
TAKE IT IN YOUR STRIDE - LEARN. REFOCUS. RE-EDUCATE YOURSELF AND SHOW THE WORLD WHAT THEY'VE BEEN MISSING!
MAKE IT HAPPEN!
SKETA

#MakeItMonday

Tuesday | 화요일 | Mardi | 星期二 | Dienstag

6

#TeamTuesday

Wednesday | 수요일 | Mercredi | 星期三 | Mittwoch

7

#WCW

8

Thursday | 목요일 | Jeidi | 星期四 | Donnerstag

#ThursdayThanks

9

Friday | 금요일 | Vendredi | 星期五 | Freitag

#FamFriday

Saturday | 토요일
Samedi | 星期六 | Samstag 10

#SaturdaySun

Sunday | 일요일
11 Dimanche | 星期日 | Sonntag

#SoulSunday

Monday | 월요일 | Lundi | 星期一 | Montag 12

Ask yourself everyday, 'What's my intention in life?' Then, get out there and make it happen!

...Sketa

#MoveMonday

Tuesday | 화요일 | Mardi | 星期二 | Dienstag 13

#TTTuesday

Wednesday | 수요일 | Mercredi | 星期三 | Mittwoch 14

#WriteWednesday

15 Thursday | 목요일 | Jeidi | 星期四 | Donnerstag

#ThoughtfulThursday

16 Friday | 금요일 | Vendredi | 星期五 | Freitag

#FlyFriday

Saturday | 토요일
Samedi | 星期六 | Samstag 17

#SuperSaturday

Sunday | 일요일
18 Dimanche | 星期日 | Sonntag

#SavourSunday

Monday | 월요일 | Lundi | 星期一 | Montag 19

Opportunities have an expiry date – just like food.
Get in early and you absorb their goodness; leave it too late and the contents spoil.
Sketa

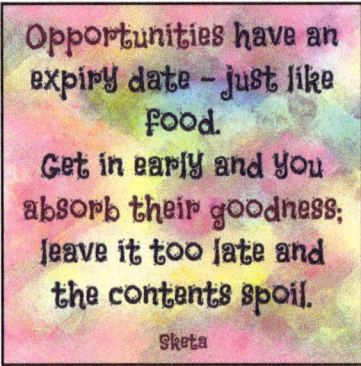

#MentorMonday

Tuesday | 화요일 | Mardi | 星期二 | Dienstag 20

#TeaTuesday

Wednesday | 수요일 | Mercredi | 星期三 | Mittwoch 21

#Watercolour

22 Thursday | 목요일 | Jeidi | 星期四 | Donnerstag

#TeachThursday

23 Friday | 금요일 | Vendredi | 星期五 | Freitag

#FunFriday

Saturday | 토요일
Samedi | 星期六 | Samstag 24

#SketchSaturday

Sunday | 일요일
25 Dimanche | 星期日 | Sonntag

#SillySunday

SEPTEMBER

Monday | 월요일 | Lundi | 星期一 | Montag 26

If it is to be,
It's up to me!
...Sketa

#MotivateMonday

Tuesday | 화요일 | Mardi | 星期二 | Dienstag 27

#TheatreTuesday

Wednesday | 수요일 | Mercredi | 星期三 | Mittwoch 28

#WorldWednesday

29

Thursday | 목요일 | Jeidi | 星期四 | Donnerstag

#TravelThursday

30

Friday | 금요일 | Vendredi | 星期五 | Freitag

#FilmFriday

Saturday | 토요일
Samedi | 星期六 | Samstag

1

#SexySaturday

2

Sunday | 일요일
Dimanche | 星期日 | Sonntag

#SleepSunday

OCTOBER

Monday | 월요일 | Lundi | 星期一 | Montag 3

A GOOD LIFE IS THINKING ABOUT THE PEOPLE AROUND YOU FIRST AND LEAVING YOU AT THE DOORSTEP.

SKETA

#MeMonday

Tuesday | 화요일 | Mardi | 星期二 | Dienstag 4

#TrumpTuesday

Wednesday | 수요일 | Mercredi | 星期三 | Mittwoch 5

#WatchMeWednesday

6

Thursday | 목요일 | Jeidi | 星期四 | Donnerstag

#TogetherThursday

7

Friday | 금요일 | Vendredi | 星期五 | Freitag

#FrameFriday

Saturday | 토요일
Samedi | 星期六 | Samstag

8

#ShopSaturday

Sunday | 일요일

9

Dimanche | 星期日 | Sonntag

#SpiritSunday

Monday | 월요일 | Lundi | 星期一 | Montag

10

NEVER JUDGE SOMEONE ELSE'S IDEA ON YOUR ABILITY TO DO OR NOT TO DO SOMETHING.

* * * * *

JUST CONGRATULATE. COLLABORATE AND CREATE WAYS TO HELP MAKE IT HAPPEN.

SKETA

#MysteryMonday

Tuesday | 화요일 | Mardi | 星期二 | Dienstag

11

#TellAllTuesday

Wednesday | 수요일 | Mercredi | 星期三 | Mittwoch

12

#WiggleWednesday

13 Thursday | 목요일 | Jeidi | 星期四 | Donnerstag

#ToDoThursday

14 Friday | 금요일 | Vendredi | 星期五 | Freitag

#FatherFriday

Saturday | 토요일
Samedi | 星期六 | Samstag 15

#SportSaturday

Sunday | 일요일
16 Dimanche | 星期日 | Sonntag

#SongSunday

OCTOBER

Monday | 월요일 | Lundi | 星期一 | Montag

17

Life will take control if you let it, you can take control if you let it...

Sketa

#MotherMonday

Tuesday | 화요일 | Mardi | 星期二 | Dienstag

18

#TryTuesday

Wednesday | 수요일 | Mercredi | 星期三 | Mittwoch

19

#WarriorWednesday

20

Thursday | 목요일 | Jeidi | 星期四 | Donnerstag

#ThrowbackThursday

21

Friday | 금요일 | Vendredi | 星期五 | Freitag

#FriendsFriday

Saturday | 토요일

Samedi | 星期六 | Samstag

22

#ShoutoutSaturday

Sunday | 일요일

23

Dimanche | 星期日 | Sonntag

#SacrificeSunday

OCTOBER

Monday | 월요일 | Lundi | 星期一 | Montag

24

NO MATTER WHAT OUR AGE, EVERYDAY SHOULD BE A LEARNING DAY.

...SKETA

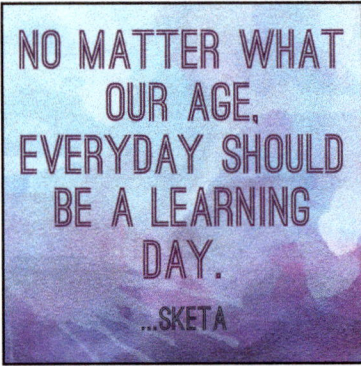

#MustDoMonday

Tuesday | 화요일 | Mardi | 星期二 | Dienstag

25

#TimeTravelTuesday

Wednesday | 수요일 | Mercredi | 星期三 | Mittwoch

26

#WednesdayWishes

27

Thursday | 목요일 | Jeidi | 星期四 | Donnerstag

#ThinkThursday

28

Friday | 금요일 | Vendredi | 星期五 | Freitag

#FameFriday

Saturday | 토요일
Samedi | 星期六 | Samstag 29

#SaveSaturday

Sunday | 일요일
30 Dimanche | 星期日 | Sonntag

#SelinaSunday

Monday | 월요일 | Lundi | 星期一 | Montag

31

JUST WHEN YOU THINK YOU HAVE WORKED OUT LIFE AND THE PEOPLE IN IT, GROUNDHOG'S DAY POPS IN AND YOU SAY TO YOURSELF, 'YUP! WON'T BE TRYING THAT, AGAIN.'

SKETA

#MakeItMonday

Tuesday | 화요일 | Mardi | 星期二 | Dienstag

1

#TeamTuesday

Wednesday | 수요일 | Mercredi | 星期三 | Mittwoch

2

#WCW

3

Thursday | 목요일 | Jeidi | 星期四 | Donnerstag

#ThursdayThanks

4

Friday | 금요일 | Vendredi | 星期五 | Freitag

#FamFriday

Saturday | 토요일
Samedi | 星期六 | Samstag

5

#SaturdaySun

6

Sunday | 일요일
Dimanche | 星期日 | Sonntag

#SoulSunday

Monday | 월요일 | Lundi | 星期一 | Montag

7

When opportunity knocks - take it with both hands! If it doesn't knock - build a big, damn door!

...Sketa

#MoveMonday

Tuesday | 화요일 | Mardi | 星期二 | Dienstag

8

#TTTuesday

Wednesday | 수요일 | Mercredi | 星期三 | Mittwoch

9

#WriteWednesday

10 Thursday | 목요일 | Jeidi | 星期四 | Donnerstag

#ThoughtfulThursday

11 Friday | 금요일 | Vendredi | 星期五 | Freitag

#FlyFriday

Saturday | 토요일
Samedi | 星期六 | Samstag 12

#SuperSaturday

Sunday | 일요일
13 Dimanche | 星期日 | Sonntag

#SavourSunday

Monday | 월요일 | Lundi | 星期一 | Montag

14

LIFE KNOWS EXACTLY, WHERE YOU ARE MEANT TO BE GOING, EVEN IF YOU DON'T.

SKETA

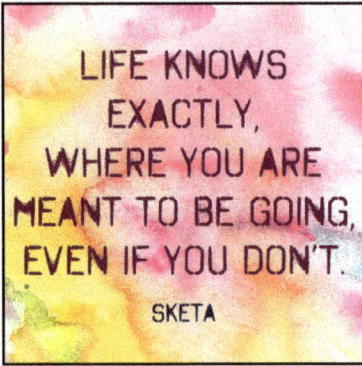

#MentorMonday

Tuesday | 화요일 | Mardi | 星期二 | Dienstag

15

#TeaTuesday

Wednesday | 수요일 | Mercredi | 星期三 | Mittwoch

16

#Watercolour

17

Thursday | 목요일 | Jeidi | 星期四 | Donnerstag

#TeachThursday

18

Friday | 금요일 | Vendredi | 星期五 | Freitag

#FunFriday

Saturday | 토요일
Samedi | 星期六 | Samstag

19

#SketchSaturday

20

Sunday | 일요일
Dimanche | 星期日 | Sonntag

#SillySunday

Monday | 월요일 | Lundi | 星期一 | Montag

21

EVERYDAY, I GIVE THANKS FOR MY LIFE; MY HEALTH, FAMILY AND FRIENDS; MY JOURNEY AND CREATOR.

SKETA

#MotivateMonday

Tuesday | 화요일 | Mardi | 星期二 | Dienstag

22

#TheatreTuesday

Wednesday | 수요일 | Mercredi | 星期三 | Mittwoch

23

#WorldWednesday

24 Thursday | 목요일 | Jeidi | 星期四 | Donnerstag

#TravelThursday

25 Friday | 금요일 | Vendredi | 星期五 | Freitag

#FilmFriday

Saturday | 토요일
Samedi | 星期六 | Samstag 26

#SexySaturday

Sunday | 일요일
27 Dimanche | 星期日 | Sonntag

#SleepSunday

NOVEMBER

Monday | 월요일 | Lundi | 星期一 | Montag

28

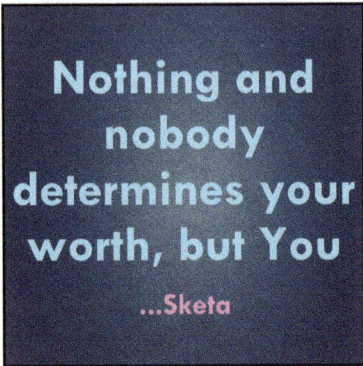

Nothing and nobody determines your worth, but You

...Sketa

#MeMonday

Tuesday | 화요일 | Mardi | 星期二 | Dienstag

29

#TrumpTuesday

Wednesday | 수요일 | Mercredi | 星期三 | Mittwoch

30

#WatchMeWednesday

1

Thursday | 목요일 | Jeidi | 星期四 | Donnerstag

#TogetherThursday

2

Friday | 금요일 | Vendredi | 星期五 | Freitag

#FrameFriday

Saturday | 토요일
Samedi | 星期六 | Samstag

3

#ShopSaturday

4

Sunday | 일요일
Dimanche | 星期日 | Sonntag

#SpiritSunday

DECEMBER

Monday | 월요일 | Lundi | 星期一 | Montag 5

ROME WASN'T BUILT IN A DAY, BUT IT WAS BUILT!

SKETA

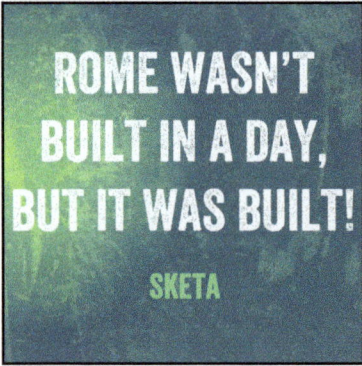

#MysteryMonday

Tuesday | 화요일 | Mardi | 星期二 | Dienstag 6

#TellAllTuesday

Wednesday | 수요일 | Mercredi | 星期三 | Mittwoch 7

#WiggleWednesday

8

Thursday | 목요일 | Jeidi | 星期四 | Donnerstag

#ToDoThursday

9

Friday | 금요일 | Vendredi | 星期五 | Freitag

#FatherFriday

Saturday | 토요일
Samedi | 星期六 | Samstag

10

#SportSaturday

11

Sunday | 일요일
Dimanche | 星期日 | Sonntag

#SongSunday

Monday | 월요일 | Lundi | 星期一 | Montag

12

Just because you do one thing today, does not mean you have to do that same one thing tomorrow - you only have today. Go out and experiment with life. Who knows, you just might find that one thing you want to do... for the **rest** of your life.

...Sketa

#MotherMonday

Tuesday | 화요일 | Mardi | 星期二 | Dienstag

13

#TryTuesday

Wednesday | 수요일 | Mercredi | 星期三 | Mittwoch

14

#WarriorWednesday

15 Thursday | 목요일 | Jeidi | 星期四 | Donnerstag

#ThrowbackThursday

16 Friday | 금요일 | Vendredi | 星期五 | Freitag

#FriendsFriday

Saturday | 토요일
Samedi | 星期六 | Samstag 17

#ShoutoutSaturday

18 Sunday | 일요일
Dimanche | 星期日 | Sonntag

#SacrificeSunday

Monday | 월요일 | Lundi | 星期一 | Montag

19

LEARN TO GIVE BEFORE YOU TAKE AND YOU WILL APPRECIATE.

SKETA

#MustDoMonday

Tuesday | 화요일 | Mardi | 星期二 | Dienstag

20

#TimeTravelTuesday

Wednesday | 수요일 | Mercredi | 星期三 | Mittwoch

21

#WednesdayWishes

22 Thursday | 목요일 | Jeidi | 星期四 | Donnerstag

#ThinkThursday

23 Friday | 금요일 | Vendredi | 星期五 | Freitag

#FameFriday

24 Saturday | 토요일
Samedi | 星期六 | Samstag

#SaveSaturday

25 Sunday | 일요일
Dimanche | 星期日 | Sonntag

#SelinaSunday

Monday | 월요일 | Lundi | 星期一 | Montag 26

YOU ARE THE DRIVER OF YOUR DESTINY. GET IN AND GIVE IT A WHIRL!

...SKETA

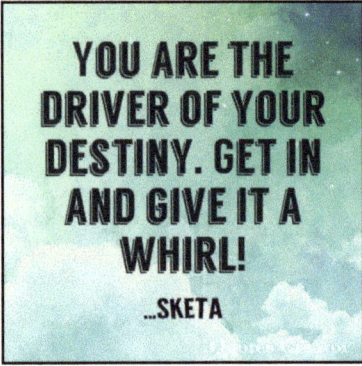

#MakeItMonday

Tuesday | 화요일 | Mardi | 星期二 | Dienstag 27

#TeamTuesday

Wednesday | 수요일 | Mercredi | 星期三 | Mittwoch 28

#WCW

29

Thursday | 목요일 | Jeidi | 星期四 | Donnerstag

#ThursdayThanks

30

Friday | 금요일 | Vendredi | 星期五 | Freitag

#FamFriday

Saturday | 토요일
Samedi | 星期六 | Samstag

31

#SaturdaySun

1

Sunday | 일요일
Dimanche | 星期日 | Sonntag

#SoulSunday

JANUARY

Monday | 월요일 | Lundi | 星期一 | Montag

2

Time appears
continuous;
even endless,
but your time is finite.
Make it count!

...Sketa

#MoveMonday

Tuesday | 화요일 | Mardi | 星期二 | Dienstag

3

#TTTuesday

Wednesday | 수요일 | Mercredi | 星期三 | Mittwoch

4

#WriteWednesday

5

Thursday | 목요일 | Jeidi | 星期四 | Donnerstag

#ThoughtfulThursday

6

Friday | 금요일 | Vendredi | 星期五 | Freitag

#FlyFriday

Saturday | 토요일
Samedi | 星期六 | Samstag 7

#SuperSaturday

8

Sunday | 일요일
Dimanche | 星期日 | Sonntag

#SavourSunday

LIFE ISN'T WHAT IT IS OR WHAT IT OFFERS: IT IS, WHAT YOU MAKE OF IT.

SKETA

Life is never just a piece of cake, Sometimes, it's just the fork.

...Sketa

Focus is Everything!

...Sketa

DON'T

RIGHT

LIFE IS V

LIFE ROCKS!

...SKETA

success
=
hard yakka +
blisters

Sketa

Build y

reali

CHANGE NEEDS CHANGE.

...SKETA

Focus is Everything!

...Sketa

EVERYDAY IS A BLESSED DAY.

...SKETA

IF YOU H

JUST C

YOU

DI

OR THE
ME OR

OU MAKE

EVERYDAY IS
A BLESSED
DAY.
...SKETA

Focus is
Everything!
...Sketa

LIFE'S NOT
MOVIN', UNLESS
IT'S MOVIN'!
...SKETA

eams a
ve in.

Sometimes,
in order to go
forward,
we need to work
out where we've
been.
Sketa

LIFE
ROCKS!
...SKETA

IPROVED
RSON'S

ADE A
CE.

Focus is
Everything!
...Sketa

Life is never just
a piece of cake,
sometimes, it's
just the fork
Sketa

LIVE A LIFE,
NOT AN
EXISTENCE.
...SKETA